W9-AUY-871
To
Ryan
From
Lisa
With Love

Yule Always Be My Friend

By Evelyn L. Beilenson and

Lois L. Kaufman

Illustrated by Jane Heyes

PETER PAUPER PRESS, INC.
WHITE PLAINS, NEW YORK

Designed by Arlene Greco

Illustrations copyright © 1999
Jane Heyes
Licensed by Wild Apple Licensing

Text copyright © 1999
Peter Pauper Press, Inc.
202 Mamaroneck Avenue
White Plains, NY 10601
All rights reserved
ISBN 0-88088-105-4
Printed in China
16 15 14 13 12 11

Visit us at www.peterpauper.com

Yule Always Be My Friend

Yule always give meaning to the words "Joy to the world."

Be my friend,
and Yule make
every day like
Christmas.

Yule make the holidays ever green.

If Yule give me the gift of friendship, it will never need pretty wrappings.

If Yule log onto the Internet we can keep our friendship on line.

Yule make
the ordinary
seem magical.

Yule wreathe
my days
in happiness.

Yule provide
the icing on
the cake
of life.

Yule be
with me
through thick
and through thin.

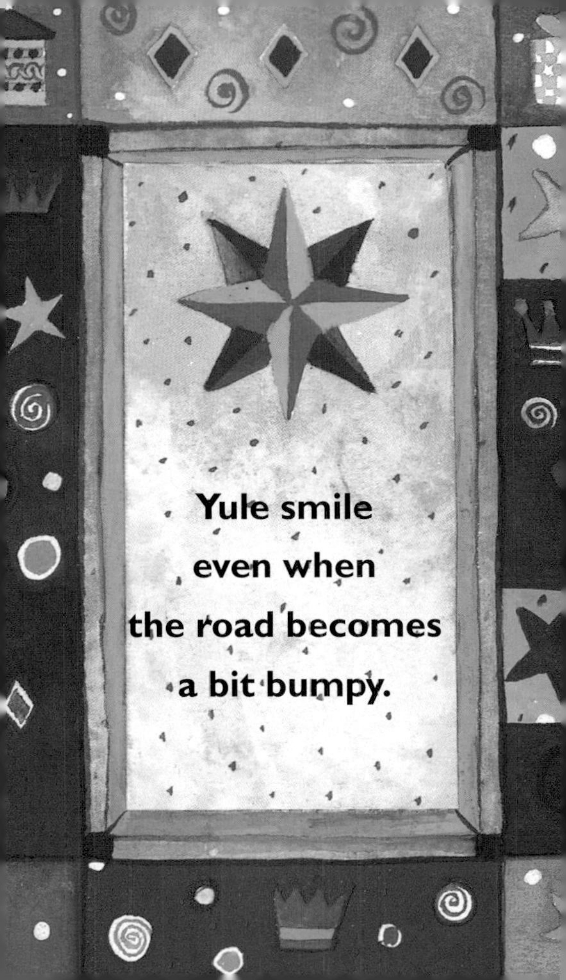

Yule smile
even when
the road becomes
a bit bumpy.

Yule strike
the spark
that lights
my life.

When necessary,
Yule always
give me that
extra pat on
the back.

Yule make
the journey
of life an incredible
adventure.

Yule encourage
only the best
in others.

Yule accept
a person's
little failures
with an open mind.

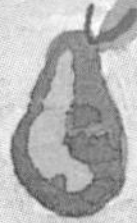

Yule never
make light of
my troubles,
but Yule help
lighten my load.

Yule make
loneliness a
distant memory.

I know Yule
always be there
for me, no matter
what I ask.

The most precious
gift Yule be able
to give is the
gift of self.

Yule help me
to take the good
with the bad
and the bad
with the good.

Yule tell me when I'm right—and also when I'm wrong.

Yule always be there to help me do things I think I can't.

When I'm feeling discouraged Yule always restore my faith in myself.

Yule help me forget the bad and remember the good.

Yule season my
life with love.

Yule always
be there to
double my joys
and divide
my sorrows.

Yule listen to
my old stories
and jokes and
never let on
you've heard them
many times before.

Yule always
know love lives
beyond the
boundaries of time.

Yule tide me
over the shoals
of life.

Yule be there
to help me to love
myself as much
as I love you.

Yule always
brighten my day
when I think
of you.

Yule never
know how much
I appreciate
your friendship.

If Yule walk
side by side with
me through life,
it will be the
perfect gift.

Yule always
bring peace
on earth to me.

Good cheer
means that
Yule be near.

I know Yule
never say
"I told you so."

If I need you in the middle of the night, I know that Yule come.

If Yule be there at the end of my journey, it will seem short to me.

If you make
a promise to me,
I know Yule
keep it.

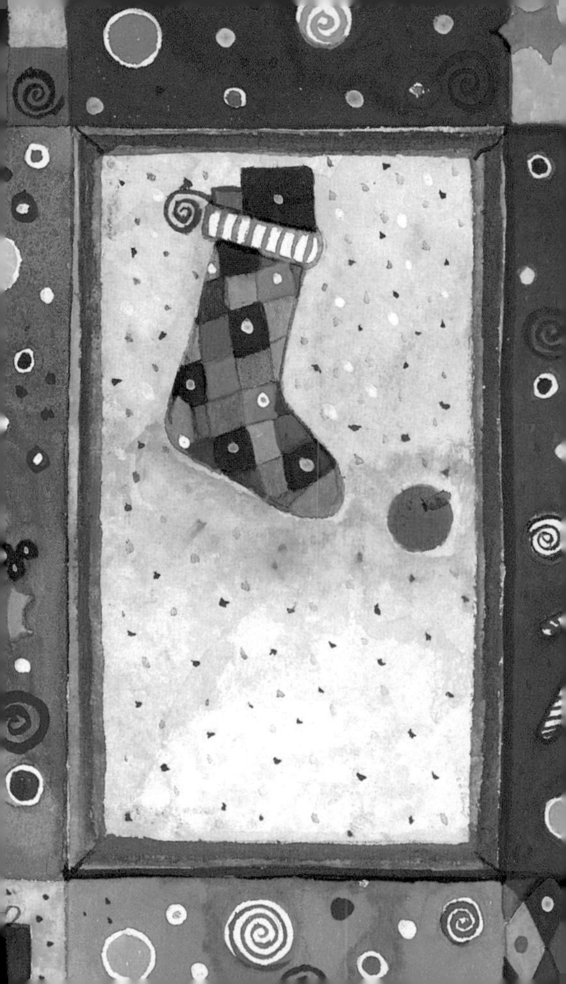

I know Yule
share my troubles,
and thus make
them half as
difficult to bear.

If Yule forgive
my faults,
we can stay
friends forever.

Yule always
keep my secrets.

I can put you
"on hold"
and know Yule
never be offended.

I know Yule
always listen
when no
one else will.

If Yule walk in the rain with me, we're sure to see a rainbow.

I know Yule
understand me,
just as I
understand you.

Yule dream

of the

future with me.

If Yule share my laughter, I'll share your tears.

I know that
Yule always
pick me up when
I'm feeling down.

I know Yule
always remember
my birthday but
forget my age.